Fantasia

Fantasia

A Collection of Poems for Children

Sumit Datta

Illustrations by: Priyadarshini Dutta and Sourojit Dutta

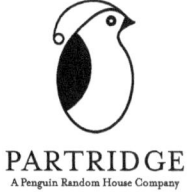

PARTRIDGE

A Penguin Random House Company

To order additional copies of this book, contact
Partridge India
000 800 10062 62
orders.india@partridgepublishing.com

www.partridgepublishing.com/india

Contents

To those for whom childhood never ends.

Brown Mountain and Blue Fountain

Brown mountain and
The blue fountain,
Love each other down there
Like an insane.

Brown mountain and
The blue fountain,
Share their joy and glory
Agony and pain.

Brown mountain and
The blue fountain,
Desiccate in dry summer
Drench up in rain.

Brown mountain and
The blue fountain,
Share floral fragrance and
Sweet pollen grain.

Brown mountain and
The blue fountain,
Share their hidden tears
Time and again.

Brown mountain and
The blue fountain,
Hug each other where red and
White flowers reign.

Brown mountain and
The blue fountain,
Kiss each other out there
In forlorn lane.

Brown mountain and
The blue fountain,
Love each other eternally
Like an insane.

Born to fly

Kite said to little bee
"I am flying high,
You cannot catch me dear
Even if you try."

Bee said "O kite
See your collar tie,
Bonded in handsome hand
I am born to fly."

Lamenting Lion

Lion was lamenting
From his core,
Gathered all creatures
Near his door.

Lion told them – his
Cubs are four,
Still they hadn't learnt
When to roar.

Lion added on
Even so more,
Leaving him lioness
Gone to sea shore.

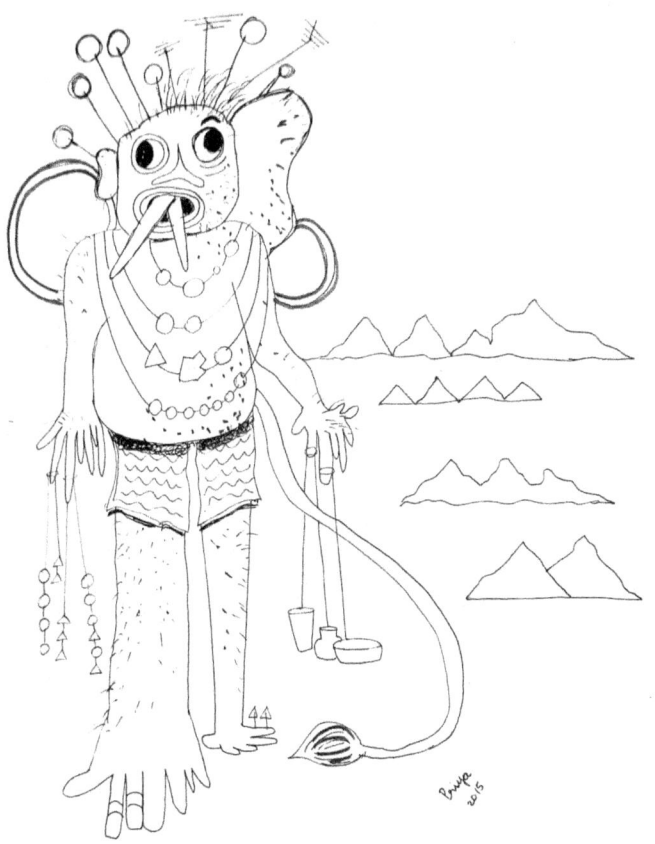

Terrohorrohoccus

Terrohorrohoccus

Terrohorrohoccus

Terrohorrohoccus lives in a lake,
Eats gold jewels and diamond flake,
When does not get,
In its own rate,
Bakes the hills and takes as cakes.

River River have you ever?

River River
Have you ever
          Gone into a tour,
Near thrilling
Hill top or
          Near azure moor?

River River
Have you ever
          Talked with a vale,
Shared your
Fantasy or
          Sweet fairy tale?

River River
Have you ever
          Danced with a bird,
Sang with her
Absurd songs
          Hitherto unheard?

River River
Have you ever
          With fullest passion,
Fallen in love
Ceaselessly
          With the blue ocean?

River River
Have you ever
        Had sweet dreams,
To fly in sky
Nudge and kiss
        Golden sun beams?

Fate of Alpine Dragon

Alpine dragon was a nonsense fool,
Never he had learned the Newton's rule.
No one sent him to a college or school
He never heard of gravity's pull,
With his body of enormous mass,
Started he suddenly hopping on grass;
One day screaming a horrible cry
Started to fly in eastern sky;
Flames all came out from his fangs,
Belly was bloated and hanged in pangs;
Suffered he lot and watch his plight
Lost all vitals in each flight.

This points to a haunting hint,
How one species can get extinct.

Dog's Day

Dog is sitting on rock of a bay,
Looking pale and dull , grim and grey;
Scratching his cheek and nudging his nose,
Grimacing towards the raven and crows.

Dog had a full belly three days past,
Since then no lunch, no breakfast;
Dog is dreaming and going in trance,
Fancying for his fairer chance.

Dog is telling his panicking pups,
'Life has too many downs and ups';
Wisely he said wise men say
'For a dog there is always a day'.

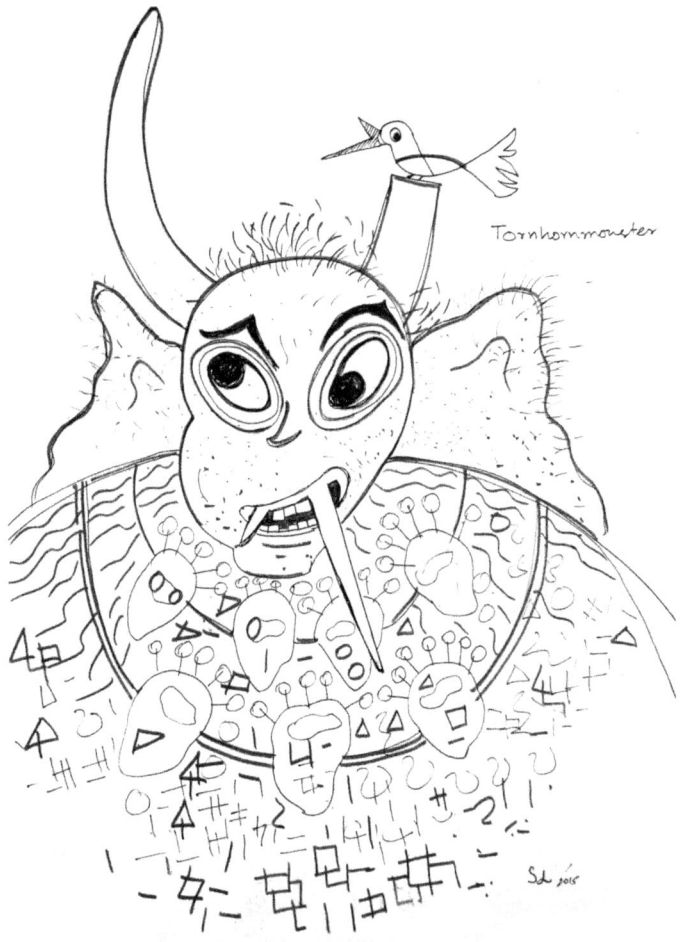

Tornhornmonster

The Tornhornmonster

Tornhornmonster

Tornhornmonster broken his horn,
In fight with one Decahecaton,
From those pieces and
Small fragments,
Hills and mountains all were born.

Teasing Breeze

Northern sea's charming breeze,
Started to tease the London bridge.
London bridge told 'leave me please,
I feel tickle and wheeze and sneeze'.

Breeze told bridge to take it with ease,
Somebody gifted the land in lease.
Lease is forever, endless seize,
No way he can leave or release.

Northern sea's charming breeze,
Tickles and teases the London bridge.
Like the dancing insane bees,
Sea breeze forever teases the bridge.

The Drama of Sky

Lightning called and told the Thunder
'I have done one very big blunder,
I have thrown some spark and light
To make all creatures cry and fright,
As I sit in sky in height
Lightly they took all my might;
Rather they tried to catch and hold,
Take my vitals in their fold.'

Thunder told 'O Lightning dear,
Who is going to run in fear'?
Call the clouds and make it dark,
And then run like a ferocious shark,
Then you start your blaze and spark,
At last I will loudly bark.'

Rain came laughing and mocked them all
'Why are you trying to frighten at all?
When the wind stops I will rain,
All your might will wash and drain'.

Sweet Abode - Haiku

Flying high in sky,
Two nest-less birds restless to
Find a sweet abode.

Orison - Haiku

The waterfowls howl
Esoteric chants and hymns
To invoke the rain.

Wintry - Haiku

Wintry fragrance of
October, wallowing in
Old poplar and pine.

The Blushing Daisy - Haiku

The blushing daisy
Concealing her smiling face
From lazy sunshine.

Songs of Sea - Haiku

Fishermen fishing,
Breeze whispering in their ear
Unheard songs of sea.

Heavenly Abode - Haiku

The red apple tree,
A heavenly abode for
Gasping wasp and bee.

The Welcome March - Haiku

Countless grasshoppers
Sprawling over brown valley,
Spring knocking on earth.

Raven's Assembly - Haiku

In banyan tree
Raven's assembly passing
Aviation bill.

Compassion - Haiku

Soul of sandy soil
Consoling dead dried leaves
Of heartless autumn.

Geometry - Haiku

Water bugs playing
Geometric zigzags over
Ripples of blue lake.

Standing Ovation - Haiku

On Kingfisher's cute
Acrobatics; fig tree gives
Standing ovation.

Funeral - Haiku

Butterfly, wasp and
Honeybee join the funeral;
The tulip is dead.

Night Drama - Haiku

Dull moon walks through sky,
Crickets cry mad in jungle,
Wolfs waiting for prey.

Nature's Poetry - Haiku

Red caterpillar
Stealthily peeling out heart
Of hazel catkin.

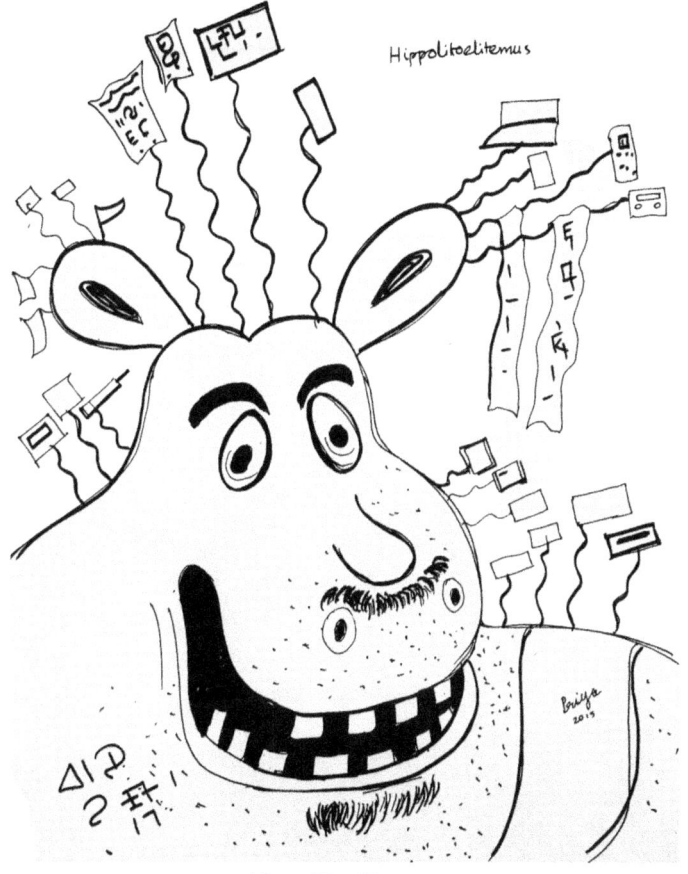

Hippolitoelitemus

Hippolitoelitemus

Hippolitoelitemus never boards in train or bus,
Hippolittoelitemus never lets the bill to pass;
Goes farer than the far,
In silver chair car,
Hippolitoelitemus eats the fate of common mass.

Butterfly

Butterfly doesn't eat butter anyway,
Butterfly flies and flutters anyway.
Runs hither runs thither, sleeps over hay,
Butterfly doesn't eat butter anyway.

Butterfly toils hard, becomes blue and grey,
Butterfly flies and flutters anyway.
Gets torn tired in torrid summer day,
Butterfly doesn't eat butter anyway.

Guess what

Fire cannot burn it, or
Water cannot wash,
Arrows cannot pierce it or
Hammers cannot crush.

Nothing like this thing you
Find on this earth,
Nothing can replace it
Nothing is it's worth.

Wind cannot blow it away
Stones cannot break,
Quakes cannot tarnish or
Storms cannot shake.

Crackers cannot crack it, or
Time cannot rust.
It has its own future
Own present past.

Nothing like this thing you
Find on this earth.
Nothing can replace it
Nothing is its worth.

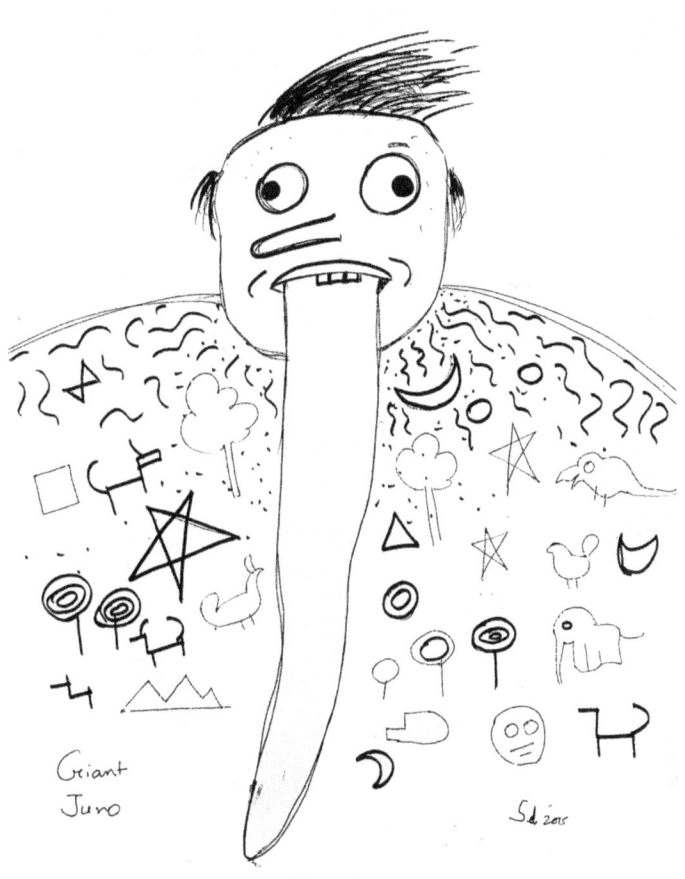

Giant Juno

Giant Juno

Giant Juno, do you know him?
Have you seen his giant face?
Do you know his father, mother?
Do you know his home address?

Giant Juno is a creature
Biggest in the universe,
From Poseidon in Macedon
He had got a cruel curse.

He will be growing, growing
Endlessly enormous,
And has to take food and drink
According to his body's mass.

Juno's father started feeding
Seedlings and smaller corn,
Juno got his tail grown up,
Grown up one brown horn.

When Juno started grazing
Under the blazing sun,
Then he started eating flowers
Eating for his fleeting fun.

Little Juno started growing
With a grim and deadly face,
Little Juno started eating
Members from other race.

Duck and hen, dog and cow,
Blue whale and elephant,
Juno started looking like a
Medieval monument.

Juno started eating forest,
River,sea and fountain,
Roaring in a deeper valley
Looking like a mountain.

Juno's father tumbled and
Started seeing horror dream,
Screaming with a grim face and
Trembled by seeing him.

Giant Juno grown further
Like a wild metaphor,
Giant Juno started eating
Tiger and Dinosaur.

"Giant Juno, Giant Juno"
Prayed all and cried all,
"Save us from this black monster
We want his downfall".

Giant Juno started eating
Earth, moon, sun and star.
Stop him somehow otherwise
Doomsdays are not so far.

Season Drama

Summer is a fiery torrid
Angry little boy,
Dallying with shiny sun
Like a tiny toy.

Autumn is a mermaid with
Sweet little fins,
Coming out digging hole in
Yellow pumpkins.

Winter is grandmother
Eighty years old,
Covering a snow blanket
Shivering in cold.

Spring is a three - winged
Singing blue bird,
Bringing all greens and reds
In the vineyard.

Rainy is a funny lad
Having no such norm,
Coming with rain cloud
Thunder and storm.

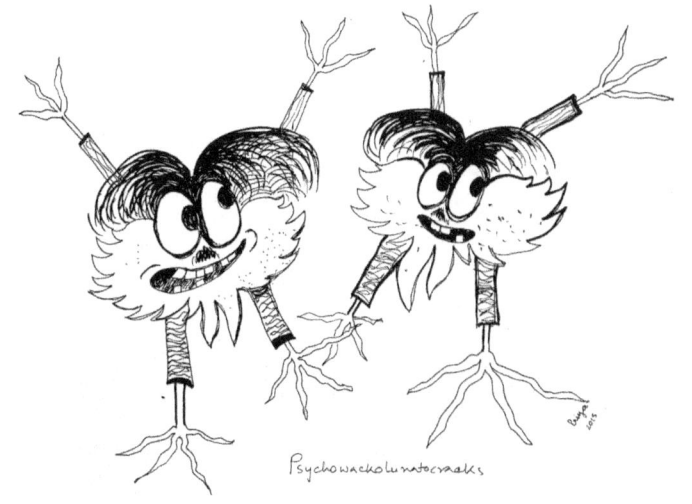

Psychowackolunatocracks

Psychowackolunatocracks

Psychowackolunatocracks,
Never run in proper tracks,
If you know their stage,
Put them in cage,
Stacking them one by one in wooden racks.

Scapegoat

One black goat
Floats on a boat,
Wearing a brownish
Ram-fur coat.

That black goat
Is writing note,
Hanging a red tie
From his throat.

Same black goat
Turned scapegoat,
When he stopped his
Ferry and float.

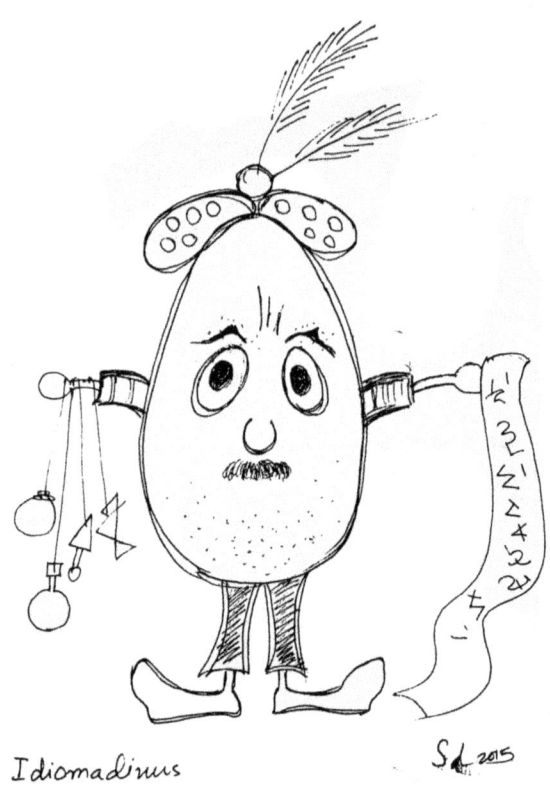

Idiomadinus

Idiomadinus

Idiomadinus

Idiomadinus is a modern day ruler,
Who sits in a room fitted with cute air cooler,
When he passes a bill,
He used to take a pill,
Given from the stocks of the greatest leg puller.

Sun and Moon

Sun is fanatic like one Hun,
Moon is lunatic like one loon,
In blue sky,
They quarrel and cry,
From mid March to the month of June.

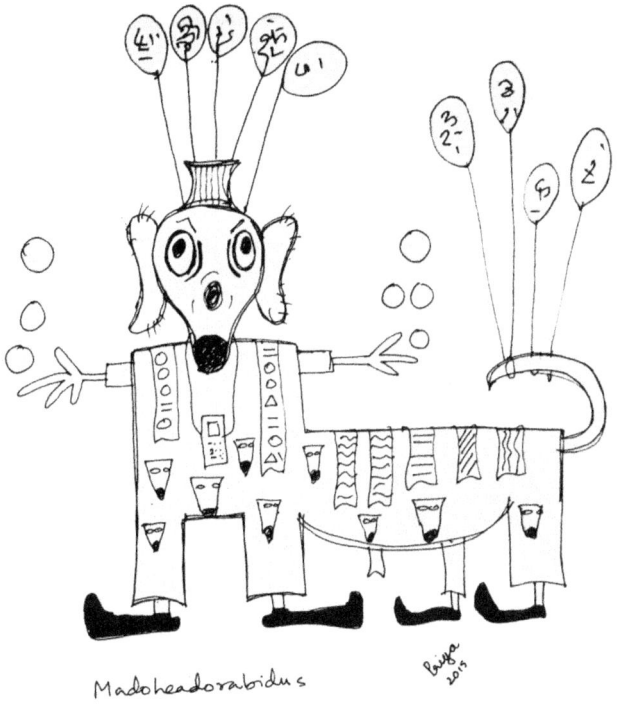

Madoheadorabidus

Madoheadorabidus

Madoheadorabidus belongs to high class,
Never walks on stone, sand or green grass,
Always makes his show,
Standing on his toe;
All his rumpuses end in big fuss.

Ostrich and Witch

Ostrich's eggs had
Fallen in a ditch,
Ostrich was crying in
Very high pitch.

Near her came one
Northern Witch,
Repaired cracks by
Magical stitch.

Ostrich gave her
Worms and leech,
Witch glutted and
Flew to sea beach.

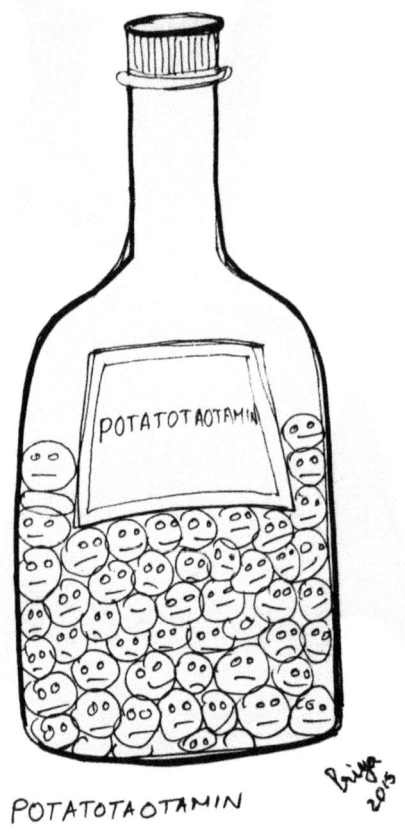

POTATOTAOTAMIN

Potatotaotamin

Potatotaotamin

Potatotaotamin is one vitamin,
Good for vision and good for rough skin,
Take money in pocket,
And buy one bucket,
It is found in fins of older dolphin.

Termite – Army

Termites are looking rude,
Crudely cutting eating wood.
Whether maple, teak or oak,
They need only tiny stroke.
Termite's great armed force,
Eating up my bed and doors.
All the old and young folk,
Cut or scratch; sneak and poke.
Are they having a filthy ploy?
To destroy my tiny 'Troy'?
Who knows my sweet home,
One day may be a wooden dome.

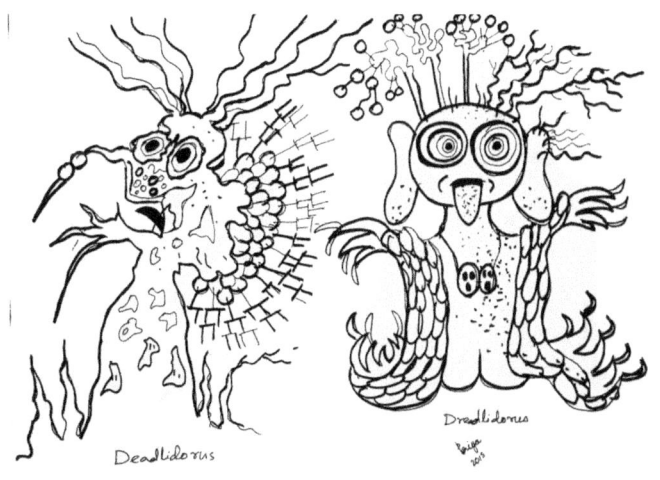

Deadlidorus and Dreadlidorus

Deadlidorus and Dreadlidorus

Deadlidorus is more ferocious than Dreadlidorus,
Deadlidorus is venomous and carnivorous.
Near the mountain,
There is a fountain,
All Deadlidoruses sit and sing song in chorus.

Giraffe's Legacy

Giraffe was telling his
Three years old,
His great grandfather's
Father was bold.

Enormously muscular and
Boundlessly tall,
Used to kick hippopotamus
Like a little ball.

Used to take water by
Dipping his full neck,
From the bottom layer of the
Tanganyika lake.

One day in fine mood in
Late afternoon,
Stretched the neck in blue sky and
Kissed the full moon.

Her Highness - The Long Hair

There was a queen, whose hair was long,
From Queensland's bridge to bay of Hong Kong,
She used to comb hair,
Sitting in a chair,
Playing her lute and singing sad song.

The Genius brain

In northern city in
Heartless lane,
There lived one
Genius brain.

Beyond the pleasure and
Beyond the pain,
Lived in solitude
Genius brain.

Traveling on his
Logical train,
Busy was in reasoning
Genius brain.

Never he looked at a
Duck or a hen,
He never walked in
Showering rain.

Shirt was torn and
Full of stain,
Searching his formula
Genius brain.

Returning home from
Southern Spain,
I, went to meet
Genius brain.

Dancing with some
Heron and crane,
Singing 'ding dong'
Genius brain.

When I asked him
What was his gain,
He took me towards a
Mud full drain.

Laughing loud in
Full disdain,
He told me all had
Gone in vain.

Riding trains in
Heartless lane,
Genius brain had
Gone insane.

Happy Hippo

Happy Hippo hops on a mud full pond,
Water glitters like white diamond,
Crow and duck,
Wish good luck,
Hippo called them in a friendship bond.

Color Play

Sedating blue and
Maddening green,
Mingled in one
Single scene.

Lawless yellow and
Reckless brown,
Sprawled on mountain
Up and down.

Umber lakes and
Violet shadow,
Kiss the soil and
Hug the meadow.

Esprit orange and
Redolent red,
Undulating in
Light and shade.

Silver water and
Golden Sun,
Having on river a
Candid fun.

Colors play here
Its own game,
No one knows it's rule
Even the name.

Demon and Lemon

Demon was sucking lemon
Like a lollypop,
Demon had stolen lemon
From the city shop.

Demon was thinking of his
Horrifying past,
Counting his homicides
And the holocaust.

Demon couldn't separate his
Good and evil deeds,
Had he done anytime
Any good indeed?

Looking at his own records
He had got a shock,
Nothing like good or holy
He had in his stock.

Demon was getting tremor
Shaking his own claws,
Perhaps he had found some
Flaws in his laws.

Demon was sucking lemon
Lemon was sour,
It may happen, lemon had a
Miraculous power.

Lemon was limy and
Lying over plate.
Can a lemon make a demon
Start contemplate?

At least the demon started
Looking his own face,
Thanks lemon, limy lemon
It is your grace.

Little Star

Don't belittle little star
Billion miles far and far,
They are as big as sun,
Never make joke or fun.
Although like a tiny drop,
They are sitting on your top;
Never laugh at them at all,
What will happen if they fall?!

www.ingramcontent.com/pod-product-compliance
Lightning Source LLC
Chambersburg PA
CBHW051238170526
45165CB00004B/1474